Heroes and Villains of the

WILD WEST

Butch Cassidy

by John Hamilton

ABDO & Daughters
PUBLISHING

Published by Abdo & Daughters, 4940 Viking Dr., Suite 622, Edina, MN 55435.

Cover Photo by: Bettmann Archive
Inside Photos by:
Bettmann Archive: pp. 5, 19, 21, 23, 27, 28
Archive Photos: pp. 9, 22
Wide World Photos: p. 17
John Hamilton: pp. 11, 12, 14, 15, 16

Edited by Ken Berg

Library of Congress Cataloging–in–Publication Data
Hamilton, John, 1959–
    Butch Cassidy / written by John Hamilton
        p. cm. — (Heroes & villains of the wild West)
    Includes bibliographical references.
    ISBN: 1-56239-560-2
1. Cassidy, Butch, b. 1866—Juvenile literature. 2. West (U.S.)—Biography—Juvenile literature. 3. West (U.S.)—History—1860–1890—Juvenile literature. 4. West (U.S.)—History—1890–1945—Juvenile literature. 5. Outlaws—West (U.S.)—Biography—Juvenile literature.
I. Title. II. Series: Hamilton, John, 1959– Heroes & villains of the wild West.
F595.C362H36 1996
978'.02—dc20   95-25039
                                                                              CIP
                                                                               AC

Contents

Butch Cassidy's First Bank Robbery

"Don't move."

The lone clerk at the San Miguel Valley Bank of Telluride, Colorado, looked up from his desk and gasped. Staring him straight in the face was the business end of a frontier pistol, the owner's finger twitching nervously on the trigger. The clerk's eyes shifted to the face of the robber. Steely blue eyes stared back with a look that could wither healthy crops in a field. The man wasn't large, but carried himself with an air of authority. People jumped when he said jump. Yet, behind the burning eyes, the clerk could see something else, a sense of humor and kindness underneath the bandit's shell. Under other circumstances, the robber was probably quite a happy-go-lucky fellow. But not today.

The bandit reached over, grabbed the clerk by the neck and pressed his face down on the desk. "Keep quiet or you're dead," the bandit said. He turned to two men hovering on the sidewalk outside the bank. "Come on, boys, it's all right!" he shouted.

As his accomplices began stuffing bags full of the bank's money, the first robber turned and looked down at the trembling clerk. Robert LeRoy Parker, alias Butch Cassidy, was disgusted with what he saw. The clerk was shaking with fright. Butch released him, and the man fell to the floor, a quivering pile of jelly.

As the three robbers slung money sacks worth about $20,000 over their shoulders, Butch turned to the clerk and said, "I've got a notion to shoot you anyway for being such a coward. Now I want you to sit there for ten minutes after we're gone. Understand?" The clerk nodded his head, his hands still raised above his shoulders. Butch strolled out of the bank

Butch Cassidy, thief, cattle rustler, well-dressed outlaw.

with his two companions. Outside the bank, the trio mounted their horses. The robbery was still undetected by the townspeople. Butch and the other two leisurely rode away, attracting no attention. Finally, after a few blocks, the bandits, whooping and hollering, fired their guns into the air and galloped off toward the countryside.

A posse was quickly formed. Although Butch had a head start, they were soon hot on his trail. Butch fired warning shots to discourage the pursuers. One deputy, upon finding himself well ahead of his companions and very close to the bandits, stopped his horse. When the rest of the posse caught up, the chase continued.

Just when the posse closed in on the bandits, Butch and his gang pulled a fast one. At the top of a large hill, a fourth bandit was waiting with fresh horses. Quickly remounting, the four sped away, leaving the posse and its winded horses in the dust. Butch's career as an outlaw was off to a roaring start.

Childhood in Utah

Robert LeRoy Parker was born on Friday, April 13, 1866, in the Mormon community of Beaver, Utah. His parents, Maxi and Ann Parker, soon moved to nearby Circleville, Utah. The family moved into a two-room cabin at the foot of the mountains and took up ranching and farming. (The cabin still stands today.)

First of 13 children, Robert Parker was a fun-loving child (he was usually up to some sort of mischief). He loved animals. He and his brothers often staged mock rodeos. As a teenager, Parker started breaking in real horses.

At first the family's cattle ranch in Circleville didn't do very well. Harsh winters devastated much of their herd. Parker's father had to buy an additional homestead, but another settler contested the right to the land. Because there were few judges on the frontier, a local bishop decided legal disputes amongst the Mormons. In this case, the bishop decided against Parker's father, who was very bitter about the ruling.

Young Parker could feel the anger in his father, and saw how the bishop's ruling hurt the family. Parker would always mistrust authority in his later days. Many point to this incident as the seed for his mistrust and wariness of large institutions and authorities like the banks, railroads, and cattle barons.

To make ends meet, Parker's mother tended a dairy herd at a nearby ranch. Parker worked as a ranch hand. Here he met Mike Cassidy, a likable drifter who was an outlaw. Cassidy soon taught the young lad all he knew about rounding up cattle, shooting a gun—and rustling. With good cause, Parker's mother was nervous about her son hanging out with Cassidy.

In the late 1800s, cattle barons ruled much of the West. Their vast herds roamed millions of acres of "public" land. Smaller ranchers and farmers resented the cattle barons. But whenever they tried to do something about it, the barons made life incredibly hard on them. It was a time when corruption was rampant, and anger ran high.

The cattle grazed on open range land. There were no fences to keep them from straying. Many times a few cattle would separate from the main herd and get lost. Other ranchers claimed these strays, giving the cattle their own brand. The reasoning was simple: how could a rancher with a herd of thousands miss a couple strays here and there, especially when they wandered miles from the main herd? This was called "mavericking," something Mike Cassidy taught young Parker how to do well. Everybody did it, even the big cattle barons. But there was a thin line between mavericking and rustling, actually stealing cattle that clearly belonged to someone else. Many young cowboys who mavericked on the side for a few extra dollars soon crossed the line—and found themselves on the wrong side of the law.

At age 17, Parker was dissatisfied with his life on the ranch. He saw no future in Utah for a young man like himself. So he left home and headed for Telluride, Colorado, looking for work.

A herd of cattle out on the open range.

Brown's Park Hideout

Parker worked for a time in and around Telluride as a ranch hand and ore hauler. Descriptions of him at this time report him as easygoing, humorous, and well liked. Business, however, was not going well. He met with new-found friends Tom McCarty and Matt Warner, both outlaws. Together, they decided to make things more exciting by robbing the local bank. Knowing the bank's layout and daily routine, the robbers had little trouble in their daring daylight raid. With advance planning, especially having a fresh set of horses waiting for them outside of town, the robbery was almost too easy. Parker's long slide into lawlessness had begun.

After the heist, the robbers split up. Parker traveled to an out-of-the-way area called Brown's Park, situated in the northwestern corner of Colorado. Lawmen hated going into this area. Gullies, canyons, caves, and unruly residents protected the outlaws. And if the law ever did catch up to the outlaws, they were soon frustrated by their quarry slipping across state lines into neighboring Utah or Wyoming, where they couldn't legally be pursued. It was easy to elude the law in this wild land, and Parker hid out successfully here for a time, working as a cowhand and farm helper.

It was while in Brown's Park that Parker changed his last name to Cassidy, after his old mentor Mike Cassidy. He did it mainly to protect his family back in Utah, but also to throw the law off his trail. Parker (now Cassidy) had a disarming way with people, and made friends everywhere he went. One Christmas he stayed with the Simpson family near the town of Lander, Wyoming, not far from Brown's Park. The children delighted in Cassidy's antics, and everybody, it seemed, adored him. He was treated like one of the family. He would in turn repay the Simpson's kindness later that winter when one of the children got severely ill. Riding alone in

The Gates of Lador, a deep canyon that lies on the south end of
Brown's Park in northwestern Colorado.

a blizzard, he made it 120 miles round trip to fetch medicine from the nearest doctor.

Cassidy soon moved on to Rock Springs, Wyoming, where he found a job at a local butcher's shop. It was here that he got him nickname "Butch." From this time on he would go by the name of Butch Cassidy.

The John Jarvie ranch in Brown's Park. Local legend says the ranch was a secret meeting place for outlaws, including Butch Cassidy.

The Wild Bunch

Butch was a natural-born leader. It wasn't long before dozens of men flocked to his side, forming the infamous band of outlaws called "The Wild Bunch." At first they stuck to cattle rustling. Butch passed himself off as a cattle trader during this time. (Many noticed, however, that Butch seldom bought, but always had cattle to sell.)

When he and his gang rode into town, the celebrations would be wild and rip-roaring. One time in Rock Springs, Colorado, the "Bunch" blazed into the Commercial Hotel. Their party was so wild someone ran to get the marshal. But before they could be arrested, the Bunch saddled up and rode out of town. The marshal, however, rode fast after them.

Cassidy glanced back and saw the marshal gaining on them. "Hurry up," Butch yelled gleefully to the marshal, timing him with a gold watch. The marshal caught up to Butch and trotted alongside. "I'll let you go," he said, "but you've got to pay a fine for the trouble you've caused in town." With that the marshal reached out and grabbed the gold watch. Butch and the Wild Bunch rode away. After all, thought Butch, fair is fair.

Hole in the Wall

Around 1890, Butch took up residence in the infamous Hole in the Wall in Wyoming. Situated about 60 miles northwest of Casper, Wyoming, the Hole in the Wall is a narrow notch, like a rifle sight, in a 50-mile-long sandstone ridge that runs north and south across the Wyoming grassland. Home to outlaws and other shady characters, it was an ideal place to rustle cattle. Hole in the Wall was the perfect defense against any lawmen foolish enough to ride into the well-protected landscape.

Butch quickly made many friends who gathered around him for leadership. Together they formed the Hole in the Wall Gang. Rustling became rampant across the countryside until finally the cattle barons

The "Wall," a 50-mile-long series of cliffs in central Wyoming that sheltered many outlaw gangs, many of whom were cattle rustlers.

"Hole in the Wall," a narrow break in the sheer sandstone cliffs.

decided to fight back. The barons launched a full-scale range war pitting their own hired guns against the small-time homesteaders and rustlers.

Cassidy's stay at Hole in the Wall was cut short. Word got to him that the law was closing in, so he packed his bags and headed across the Bighorn Mountains for the Wind River Basin area of Wyoming. There he stayed in a cabin with friend Al Hainer. But not for long. Detectives hired by the cattle barons soon tracked Butch down and arrested him on April 11, 1892.

Cassidy was hauled in to jail on charges of buying stolen horses. He got two years in prison, a sentence that made him very bitter. After serving half his sentence, Wyoming Governor W. A. Richards pardoned the model prisoner if he promised not to steal horses or rob banks ever again in Wyoming. Butch promised, and was soon released.

Prison was a low point in Butch's life. His stay at the Wyoming State Penitentiary made him a more hardened criminal. After walking away from the prison, Butch decided that if he was going to be an outlaw, he was going to be the most feared and dreaded outlaw in the West.

Cassidy returned to Hole in the Wall and soon teamed up with his old gang, including longtime friend Elzy (pronounced El-zuh) Lay, and Harry Longabaugh, alias the Sundance Kid. (The Kid got his nickname after a stint in prison in Sundance, Wyoming.) Like Butch, Sundance was a lightning-quick crack shot, and had a soft spot for the underdog. Unlike Butch, however, he could be reserved and had a short temper. Still, he and Butch quickly became good friends.

This narrow canyon, just west of Hole in the Wall, contains the "bandit's cave," a hideout believed to have been used at one time by Butch Cassidy and his Hole in the Wall Gang.

Harry Longabaugh (the Sundance Kid) with his girlfriend, Etta Place.

The Montpelier Bank Robbery

On August 13, 1896, Butch, Elzy Lay and another robber called Bub Meeks rode into the town of Montpelier, Idaho. On that hot day, Butch and Elzy strode into the bank, leveled their six-shooters and shouted, "Put up your hands. Don't make a sound. This is a stickup!"

As Elzy Lay stuffed bills and gold into sacks, Butch kept his gun trained on the customers and bank tellers. (The customers, though trembling with fear, needn't have worried. Butch never killed a soul in any of his robberies, and never stole the personal possessions of common people.) Bub Meeks held the outlaws' horses just outside.

The work was done quickly. The bandits strode outside to their horses, mounted, and casually rode out of town. A natural actor, Cassidy fooled many people with this calm performance. Once on the city outskirts, the robbers broke into a hard gallop, for they knew a posse would soon be hot on their trail. Just like in the Telluride bank robbery, however, Butch had the foresight to station fresh horses several miles away. The posse never caught up to the bandits, who rode away with about $20,000 in loot.

That winter the gang stayed in a cabin hideout at Robbers' Roost, another canyon-filled stronghold, this one situated in the high desert country of southeastern Utah.

Banks weren't the only target for Cassidy and his gang. On April 21, 1897, in Castle Gate, Utah, Butch shoved his gun into the face of the paymaster at the Pleasant Valley Coal Company and relieved him of his pay satchel with nearly $9,000 inside. But the money made from these robberies wasn't nearly enough to satisfy Butch and the rest of the Wild Bunch. So, they decided to try something different next time: train robbery.

A young Butch Cassidy in an undated photograph.

 19

The Wilcox Train Robbery

Cassidy knew that big money could be had by robbing trains, since bank and cattle baron money was often transported on these "iron horses." On June 2, 1899, armed robbers stopped the Overland Flyer of the Union Pacific Railroad near Wilcox, Wyoming. (Butch's promise to the governor evidently didn't include trains.)

Surrounding the express car, Cassidy called for the guard inside, a man named E.C. Woodcock, to open the locked door. Woodcock refused, despite much cursing and threats. "Come in and get me!" Woodcock stubbornly shouted. In reply, the robbers blew up the door with dynamite,

In 1899, Butch and his gang began robbing trains.

A boxcar filled with members of the "super posse" that pursued Butch Cassidy and the Wild Bunch. The posse was employed by Pinkerton's National Detective Agency. Their motto was, "We never sleep."

 21

blasting open a huge hole in the side of the car and knocking Woodcock unconscious. One of the robbers wanted to kill Woodcock, but Butch said, "Leave him be. A man with his nerve deserves not to be shot."

Since the only man who knew the safe's combination was now unconscious, the robbers were forced to blow it up also. The blast blew off the safe door and completely wrecked the express car. The bandits had to scamper around the tracks, picking up all the money that flew into the air from the explosion. Their take was impressive: nearly $30,000.

In the months to come, several train robberies fit this same pattern, undoubtedly masterminded by Butch. On August 29, 1900, the gang stopped another Union Pacific train near Tipton, Wyoming, and again

Allan Pinkerton

encountered Mr. Woodcock. This time, Woodcock decided to open the door without getting blown up. The robbers made off with more than $50,000.

It was the last straw for the Union Pacific Railroad. They were determined to put a stop to the train robberies once and for all. The railroad hired the Pinkerton Agency, a private group of detectives well known for tracking down outlaws. They formed a "super posse" of over 100 marksmen—some of them the best shots in the West—to hunt down Cassidy and the Wild Bunch. The super posse was even given a special train. They were outfitted with whatever weapons and supplies they needed, and paid very well. Butch's days as an outlaw were numbered.

Cassidy and his gang managed to escape to Texas, but life on the run was beginning to wear out the 34-year-old outlaw leader. He had been on the wrong side of the law for over 11 years, and spent two years behind bars. He knew that time was running out on the era of the Wild West. Trains and telegraphs seemed to make the country smaller, and certainly made it more difficult to hide out after a robbery. Butch decided South America offered more safety from the long arm of the law.

But first, Butch needed to pull off one last score. On September 19, 1900, he and the Sundance Kid arrived in the town of Winnemucca,

Left to right, standing: William Carver ("He smelled like a skunk."), Harvey Logan (Kid Curry); *sitting,* Harry Longabaugh (The Sundance Kid), Ben Kilpatrick (The Tall Texan), Robert Parker (Butch Cassidy).

Nevada. Outlaw Bill Carver followed them into town. Unfortunately, on the way to town, Carver had a run-in with a skunk, which got the best of him. During the robbery, Cassidy, Sundance and the citizens in the bank nearly choked to death before the theft was finished. The robbers made a safe getaway with over $30,000. Wanted posters for the holdup described Carver as "having a very determined face and smelling like a polecat."

After escaping to Texas, Butch and several gang members posed for a portrait in which they were all decked out like city slickers. He sent a copy to the bank in Winnemucca, thanking them for their contribution. Cassidy thought it was a grand joke.

"Bandidos Yanqui"

With the Pinkertons still hot on his trail, Butch was determined to skip the country. He talked it over with Sundance, and together they decided to meet in New York City. When they met, Sundance had his girlfriend, Etta Place, with him. At first, Butch wasn't wild about bringing the adventure-loving schoolteacher along. However, Sundance finally convinced him to let her come. After spending several days dining and drinking in Manhattan, the trio set sail for Argentina.

The facts are sketchy about Butch's days in South America. Record keeping was poor, and Cassidy undoubtedly moved from place to place quite often. It is known he worked for a time as a ranch hand, and also did a stint working for a tin mine in Bolivia. He and Sundance were also quite likely responsible for several bank robberies in Bolivia and Argentina. (Local authorities began issuing reports of a pair of mysterious American cowboy bank robbers. They called them the "Bandidos Yanqui," or Yankee Bandits.) But, like in the United States, identification was difficult. The pair were probably blamed for many more robberies than they actually committed.

In 1906 Sundance brought Etta back to the United States because she had become very ill. Some time later, he returned to South America on his own, where he once again linked up with Butch. Together, they set out for Bolivia. For the two seasoned outlaws, the small South American country had banks ripe for the picking.

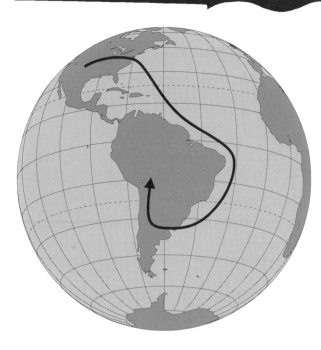

Fleeing South of the Border

With the Pinkerton Agency hot on their trail, Butch Cassidy and the Sundance Kid left the American West and headed to South America. After a brief stop in New York City, they traveled to Argentina and Bolivia, where they continued their bank-robbing ways.

ARGENTINA

Buenos Aires

Bolivia

Lake Titicaca

■ La Paz

■ San Vicente

■ Sucre

End of an Outlaw

According to Pinkerton records (they were still keeping track of Cassidy, even in South America), the two Yankee outlaws continued their robberies until 1908, when they were trapped near San Vicente, Bolivia, by a company of soldiers. As the story goes, Butch and Sundance made a dash for their rifles and were fired upon by the soldiers. They made it back to a shack, but Sundance was mortally wounded. Vowing never to be taken alive, Butch put Sundance out of his misery, then turned his pistol, with one last bullet in the chamber, on himself. Later, the two outlaws were buried in a small cemetery on the outskirts of town. Butch Cassidy had finally met his maker.

Or had he? Convincing evidence leads many to believe that Butch made it back to the United States. After his widely believed "death" in Bolivia, he could finally start a new chapter in his life, putting aside his bandit ways and settling down. Some believe Cassidy changed his name to William Phillips and lived out the remainder of his life in Spokane, Washington. Handwriting analysis, plus eyewitnesses who swear they saw Butch after his supposed death, seem to support this claim.

Lula Parker Betenson, Cassidy's sister, also claimed that her brother made it back alive. She said he visited the family in Utah in 1925. (But he was not, she said, William Phillips.) According to his sister, Butch died somewhere in the Northwest in 1937.

We may never know whether Butch Cassidy ever made it back to his beloved Wild West. Somehow it seems fitting to think that one of the last of the Old West outlaws—a gentleman robber who probably never killed anyone—returned home to finally rest in peace.

Lula Parker Betenson, Butch Cassidy's sister. She claims Butch returned to the United States, visited the family, and lived to a ripe old age.

The Wild West of Butch Cassidy

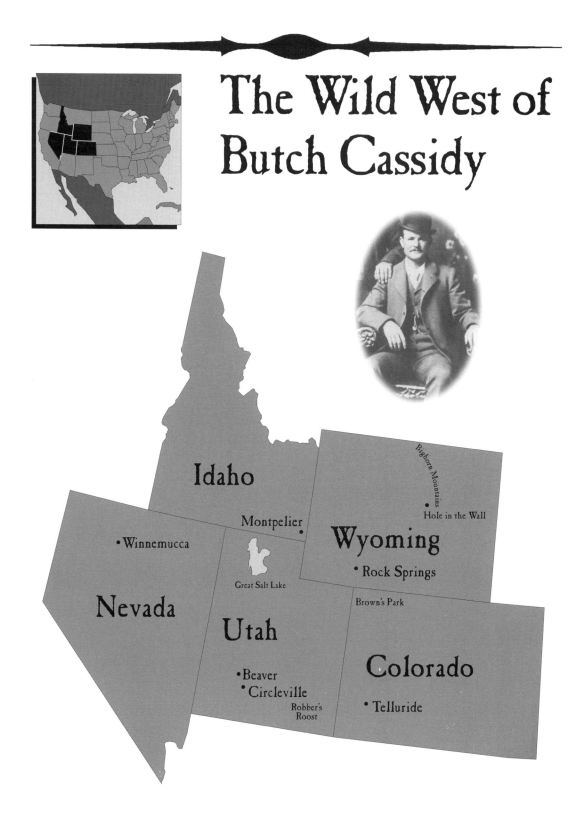

Idaho

Montpelier

• Winnemucca

Great Salt Lake

Nevada

Utah

• Beaver
• Circleville

Robber's
Roost

Bighorn Mountains

• Hole in the Wall

Wyoming

• Rock Springs

Brown's Park

Colorado

• Telluride

Glossary

cattle baron

A person who, honestly or by twisting the law, becomes the owner of huge sections of rangeland and has his brand on a large herd of cattle. The term was usually meant as a sort of insult, but many honest and well-respected men were referred to as cattle barons.

dynamite

A powerful explosive (composed of nitroglycerin or ammonium nitrate) usually made into stick form, with a fuse on one end. Butch Cassidy sometimes used dynamite to blast open railroad cars and safes.

homestead

Land claimed by a settler under a law called the Homestead Act. This law encouraged pioneers to settle in the Western states. The Homestead Act, passed in 1862, promised ownership of 160 acres of land to families if they cleared and improved upon it, and lived there for at least five years.

marshal

Frontier towns elected their own police forces, including a "marshal." Marshals were sworn to see that all laws were observed, and to keep the peace. They often hired assistants, called 'constables' or 'assistant marshals.' Some famous marshals of the Old West included James Butler "Wild Bill" Hickok, Wyatt Earp, and Bat Masterson.

mavericking

To take possession of unbranded cattle on the open range. In the days before fences were widely used, many strays roamed the vast landscape. It was perfectly legal to round these strays up and add them to a rancher's herd. (See also, *rustling*.)

Mormon

A member of the Church of Jesus Christ of Latter-day Saints. The Mormon religion was founded in 1830 by Joseph Smith. In the mid-1800's, church leader Brigham Young led a huge number of Mormon followers out West. Most settled in what is now called Utah, where Butch Cassidy was born and raised.

Pinkerton, Allan (1819–1884)

Scottish-born American detective and Civil War spy. In 1850 he started Pinkerton's National Detective Agency. He became famous after discovering a plot to murder Abraham Lincoln in 1861. During the Civil War he organized the Secret Service of the U.S. Army.

posse

A number of citizens who are given legal authority to round up criminals.

rustling

To steal cattle. As opposed to "mavericking," a legal activity where unbranded cattle on the open range are rounded up and added to a rancher's herd. Stealing cattle that were already marked with another rancher's brand was a serious crime in the Old West. Cattle thieves were often shot or hanged. (See also, *mavericking*.)

Union Pacific Railroad

The railroad company that built the first rail line linking the East and West Coasts. On May 10, 1869, locomotives from the Eastern and Western United States linked up in Promontory, Utah, creating the first transcontinental railroad. This rail line opened the West to supplies from both coasts, and became a major means of transportation for settlers of the Old West.

Bibliography

Baker, Pearl. *The Wild Bunch at Robbers Roost.* New York: Abelard-Schuman, 1971.

Betenson, Lula Parker. *Butch Cassidy, My Brother.* Provo, Utah: Brigham Young University Press, 1975.

Flanagan, Mike. *Out West.* New York: Harry N. Abrams, Inc., 1987.

Horan, James D. *The Outlaws: The Authentic Wild West.* New York: Crown Publishers, Inc., 1977.

Nash, Jay Robert. *Bloodletters and Badmen.* New York: M. Evans and Company, 1973.

Pointer, Larry. *In Search of Butch Cassidy.* Norman, Oklahoma: University of Oklahoma Press, 1977.

Redford, Robert. *Riding the Outlaw Trail.* National Geographic, November, 1976, pp. 622-657.

Steckmesser, Kent Ladd. *Western Outlaws.* Claremont, California: Regina Books.

Index